United States of America
ISBN 978-1933878133
Copyright © 2010 Jill Rossiter

DW
Publishing Co.

For Sales

Including

Educational Discounts:

Email, fax, or phone how many of which
book you would like and we will reply with
a quotation and order form.

2337 SE Master Ave.
Port Saint Lucie FL 34952
Phone: (863) 425-1659
Fax: (772) 934-3528

Email: Orders@DWPublishingCo.com

I

Table of Contents

I. Introduction
About this Book 1
What is APA Style? 1

II. Getting Started
General Guidelines 2
Plagiarism 3
What to Document 3
What Not to Document 3
Before You Begin 4
Information to Record 4-6

III. Format
Page Types 7
General Format 8-9
Title Page 10-11
Abstract 12-13
Text Page(s) 14-15
References Page(s) 16-17

IV. In-Text Documentation
Basic In-text Documentation 18-19
Placement of In-Text Documentation 19-20
Documenting Paragraphs 20-21
Long Quotations 22
Common Problems 23-28

V. Common Style Issues 29-31

VI. References Page(s)
Guidelines for References 32
  Digital Object Identifiers 33-34
  DOI References 34
  DOI Common Problems 34
Books 35-37
  Common Problems 37-39

Journals
  Journals 40-43
  Magazine 44-45
  Newspaper 45-46
  Common Problems 46-48

Online and Electronic Resources 49-50
  Other Resources 53-53
  Audiovisual Materials 53-56
  Reviews 56

VII. Additional Resources 57

VIII. Index 58-59

Introduction

About this Book

In this book we utilize real, viable sources for our examples. We do not create examples to fit the models. Your sources will not always fit the models provided; we understand that and do our best to offer examples that demonstrate real-life situations.

What is APA Style?

Created and maintained by the American Psychological Association, APA style is a system used to prepare manuscripts for publication. It is also used to document the results of one's own research. More details on how to prepare manuscripts and present research are available in the *Publication Manual of the American Psychological Association*.

More generally, high school and college teachers often require APA documentation for general research papers. This book is designed to help those writers.

Many students are frustrated by APA because it doesn't seem to follow what most of us would consider "logical," "normal" rules. Perhaps most noticeably, the capitalization in APA is not traditional, and documentation emphasizes publication dates. However, with a good guidebook like this one, you can master APA documentation.

General Guidelines:

The most important point to remember when working in APA is to **be consistent**. A person reading (and perhaps grading) your essay will be less likely to see errors if your work is consistent. Students lose points when they use a comma at the end of the author's name in one place and a period in the next. The reader may not know which is correct, but the lack of consistency will highlight the error.

When compiling your references, you may not find an exact model for your source. When in doubt, use the model that is closest to your situation, and supplement this book with the Internet sites listed on the last page.

Don't expect to memorize APA documentation and be done with it. You probably won't remember all of the rules all of the time. Use the models each time you create a new entry.

Finally, be wary of Internet sites and software that format your sources for you. While these can be helpful, they can also produce bibliographies riddled with errors. Do the work yourself to ensure that it is correct.

Plagiarism

Plagiarism is a serious offense in any academic setting. As few as three or four words in a row taken directly from a source can be considered plagiarism.

You can plagiarize in two ways: by plagiarizing words or by plagiarizing ideas. When you use other people's words or ideas in your writing, you must acknowledge the source. Never copy words directly from your source without enclosing them in quotation marks and including documentation. If you don't acknowledge that the words or ideas came from someone else, you have plagiarized.

APA also warns against self-plagiarism. This means taking information that you have already published and presenting it as new scholarship.

What to Document:

Any thought that did not come from your head requires documentation. This includes both ideas (individual ideas, summaries or paraphrases) and direct quotations.

What Not to Document:

*Your own ideas
*Common knowledge
*Very general information found in a variety of sources
(The White House is located at 1600
Pennsylvania Ave. in Washington, D.C.)

Before You Begin:

Read the instructions carefully. Specific requirements can vary; for example, some instructors will not require an abstract. Ask for clarification if you don't understand any of the specific instructions. It is vital to understand your assignment before you begin.

Begin your research by taking good notes. As you find your sources, record the information you will need in order to document them. See the chart on pages 5 & 6.

It is a good idea to do the majority of your research before you begin writing. Your research should represent different points of view on your topic, including those of the best-known scholars in your topic area. If you read your sources before you write, you can speak comprehensively on your topic. Find additional sources as you need them.

Information to Record:

Following are lists of information you may need in order to document your sources. You should record as much information as is available.

Getting Started - Information to Record

For an Anthology:
- author of the section or chapter (last name and initials)
- year of publication (the anthology)
- section or chapter title
- book title
- section or chapter page number(s)
- edition (if other than 1st)
- city where published
- publisher
- if a direct quote, record the page number(s) for each quote

For a Book:
- author's last name and initials
- year of publication
- book title
- edition (if other than 1st)
- city where published
- publisher
- if a direct quote, record the page number(s) for each quote

For a Journal (paper copy):
- author's last name and initials
- title of article
- title of journal
- year of publication
- volume and issue or number if available
- page numbers

Getting Started - Information to Record

For a Journal (electronic):
- author's last name and initials
- title of article
- title of journal and year of publication
- volume and issue or number if available
- home page URL OR name of database and entry URL
- page numbers if available
- Digital Object Identifier (DOI) if available

For a Personal Communication (e-mail, interview):
- full name of interviewee
- date of interview
- take good notes (make sure quotes are exact)

For an Internet document:
- author's last name and initials
- year of last update or publication
- title of the page
- Internet address

*Only classify a source as an Internet document if the source does not fit one of the other categories.

Format - Page Types

Page Types:

Your paper will consist of four types of pages:

Title Page

Running head: MULTIPLE INTELLIGENCES   1

Multiple Intelligences Theory

in Primary Education

Carol A. Wykis

Lewis-Clark State College

Abstract Page

MULTIPLE INTELLIGENCES   2

Abstract

Multiple Intelligences Theory, developed by Howard Gardner, suggests that individuals have varying levels of intelligence in different areas. These intelligences include: linguistic, logical-spatial, kinesthetic, musical, interpersonal, and intrapersonal, and natural. Today's classrooms are utilizing this theory by having students for strengths and weaknesses in each area, and using that knowledge to teach more effectively. Because all intelligences are so closely related, learning is one area can increase intelligence in all areas.

Text Page(s)

MULTIPLE INTELLIGENCES   3

Multiple Intelligences Theory
in Primary Education

Jason was a seven boy, with a gentle spirit and a knack for conversation. Unfortunately, he strued poorly on tests, and teachers were disappointed with his below-average daily work. His parents saw a different side of Jason. When they studied with him at home, Jason seemed to understand concepts as he perused the content. His parents couldn't understand why he was failing in school. Like so many struggling students, Jason would have benefited from instruction based on Multiple Intelligences Theory.

Howard Gardner introduced his Multiple Intelligences Theory in 1983. Originally, Gardner listed seven intelligences (linguistic, logical-mathematical, musical, spatial, bodily-kinesthetic, interpersonal, and intrapersonal), but later added naturalist, for a total of eight. By applying this theory in the education system, we can identify individual students' strengths and weaknesses, and help them learn more effectively.

The first intelligence is linguistic. Students strong

References Page(s)

MULTIPLE INTELLIGENCES   13

Reference

Almera, M. (2004, Fall). An intelligent use for belief *Frames of mind: Theory of Multiple Intelligences by Howard Gardner*. In *Education 127*, 40(3). Retrieved from http://find.galegroup.com/itomo/start

Educational Broadcasting Corporation. (2004). *Concept to classroom: Tapping into Multiple Intelligences*. Retrieved from http://www.thirteen.org/edonline/concept2class/index.html

Gardner, H. (1983). *Frames of mind: The theory of Multiple Intelligences*. New York: Basic Books.

Gardner, H., Kornhaber, M.L., & Wake, W.K. (1996). *Intelligence: Multiple perspectives*. Fort Worth, TX: Harcourt Brace College Publishers.

Nelson, J.L. (2001, Fall). Multiple intelligences in the classroom: Characteristics of the eight types of intelligence, is identified by Howard Gardner. In *Education 124*, 123(5). Retrieved from http://find.galegroup.com/itomo/start

Shearer, B. (2004, January). Multiple Intelligences Theory after 20 years. In *Teachers College Record*, 106 1-6. Retrieved from http://find.galegroup.com/itomo/start

General Format Rules:

The general format rules are as follows:

- Use standard 8½" x 11" white paper.
- Use a 12 point Times New Roman font.
- Place a running head and the page number ½" from the top of every page.
- For the body of the text, apply 1" margins top, bottom, and on both sides.
- Double space throughout the text.

The running head and page number:

A running head is a shortened version of your title, printed on the left-hand margin at the top of each page (including the title page). It should be no longer than 50 characters including punctuation and spaces. Begin on the left margin 1/2" from the top of the page.

The title page includes the words "Running head" (capital R, lower case h), a colon, a space, and the running head in upper-case letters (ALL CAPS). All subsequent pages should include the running head on the top left side of the page without the words "Running head." The page number should be on the right margin of the same line. Use the number 1 on the title page and continue numbering pages throughout the paper, including References page(s).

General Format

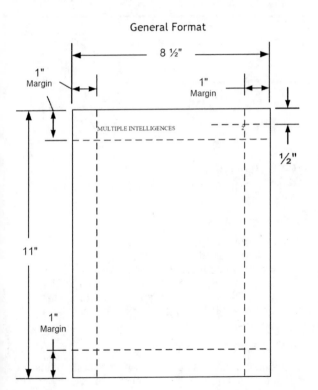

MULTIPLE INTELLIGENCES

8 ½"

1" Margin

1" Margin

½"

11"

1" Margin

Title Page:

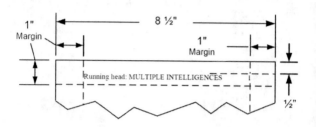

Running head: MULTIPLE INTELLIGENCES

1" Margin · 8 ½" · 1" Margin · ½"

Running head:
Begin with the running head and page number as shown above.

Title:
Make your title concise but telling. Avoid abbreviations and words with little meaning. The title should be no more than 12 words in length. Capitalize the first letter of the first word and all major words. Do not underline or use bold. Center the title horizontally and place it on the top half of the page.

Author's name/byline:
Double space and give your name (first, middle initial and last name). Do not use the word "by."

Format - Title Page

Institution/affiliation:

Double space and give the na[me of the] institution where the research wa[s done. If the] author has no affiliation, give the [city and state of] the author's residence. Do not use the word ...

Your final title page should look like this:

Multiple Intelligences Theory

in Primary Education

Carol A. Wylds

Lewis-Clark State College

---

ract Page:

The abstract is a brief summary of the contents of your paper. It is necessary for publication and usually required by instructors. If you are in doubt about whether or not you need one, include it. APA does not give a specific limit, but notes that some journals limit abstracts to 150 words.

The abstract should begin at the top of the second page. Start with your running head and page number. Next type the word "Abstract" centered, along the top margin (still using one inch margins). Double space and begin your abstract. Do not indent. Do not include anything else on this page.

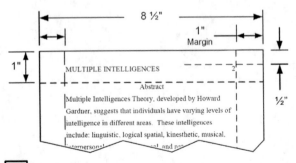

Format - Abstract Page

Your final abstract page should look like this:

MULTIPLE INTELLIGENCES   2

Abstract

Multiple Intelligences Theory, developed by Howard Gardner,
suggests that individuals have varying levels of intelligence in
different areas. These intelligences include: linguistic, logical
spatial, kinesthetic, musical, interpersonal, and intrapersonal, and
natural. Today's educators are utilizing this theory by testing
students for strengths and weaknesses in each area, and using that
knowledge to teach more effectively. Because all intelligences
are so closely related, learning in one area can increase
intelligence in all areas.

Text Page(s):

The First Page:

On the first page of your essay, as on every other page, include the running head and page number (see instructions on pages 8-10). Repeat the full title just as it appears on the title page (1 inch from the top, centered, and using the same capitalization). Double space and begin the body of your essay.

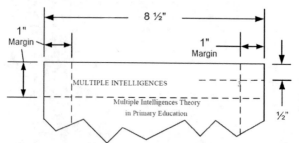

The Text Body:

Indent the first line of each paragraph five to seven spaces (be consistent). Use left justification only, and do not hyphenate words on the right-hand margin. Continue with the running head, page number, and 1 inch margins throughout the paper. Double space the entire body of the paper (including quotes).

14

Format - Text Page(s)

Your first text page should look this:

MULTIPLE INTELLIGENCES   3

Multiple Intelligences Theory

in Primary Education

Jason was a sweet boy with a gentle spirit and a
knack for conversation. Unfortunately, he scored
poorly on tests, and teachers were disappointed with his
below-average daily work. His parents saw a different
side of Jason. When they studied with him at home,
Jason seemed to understand concepts as he prepared for
exams. His parents couldn't understand why he was
failing in school. Like so many struggling students,
Jason would have benefited from instruction based on
Multiple Intelligences Theory.

Howard Gardner introduced his Multiple
Intelligences Theory in 1983. Originally, Gardner listed
seven intelligences (linguistic, logical-mathematical,
musical, spatial, bodily-kinesthetic, interpersonal, and
intrapersonal), but later added naturalist, for a total of
eight. By applying this theory to the education system,
we can identify individual students' strengths and
weaknesses, and help them learn more effectively.

The first intelligence is linguistic. Students strong

Note: Your remaining text pages should not display the title.

References Page(s):

The first page of References should be a separate piece of paper after the last page of your text.

Center the word "References" immediately below the top margin.

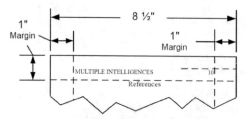

Double space and begin listing your sources. List your sources alphabetically by the author's last name. Double space all entries and <u>indent all entry lines except the first line</u> (known as "hanging indent").

For specific instructions on References, see Guidelines for References (page 32).

Format - References Page(s)

Your first page of References should look this:

MULTIPLE INTELLIGENCES   11

References

Aborn, M. (2006. Fall). An intelligent use for belief. *Frames of
      mind: Theory of Multiple Intelligences* by Howard
      Gardner. In *Education, 127,* 83(3). Retrieved from
      http://find.galegroup.com/menu/start

Educational Broadcasting Corporation. (2004). *Concept to
      classroom: Tapping into Multiple Intelligences.* Retrieved
      from http://www.thirteen.org/edonline/concept2class/mi/
      index.html

Gardner, H. (1983). *Frames of mind: The theory of Multiple
      Intelligences.* New York: Basic Books.

Gardner, H., Kornhaber, M. L., & Wake, W. K. (1996).
      Intelligence: Multiple perspectives. Fort Worth, TX:
      Harcourt Brace College Publishers.

Nolen, J. L. (2003. Fall). Multiple intelligences in the
      classroom: Characteristics of the eight types of
      intelligences as identified by Howard Gardner. In
      Education, 124, 115(5). Retrieved from
      http://find.galegroup.com/menu/start

Shearer, B. (2004, January). Multiple Intelligences Theory after
      20 years. In *Teachers College Record, 106,* 2-6. Retrieved
      from http://find.galegroup.com/menu/start

Additional pages of References will not
display the "References" heading.

Basic In-Text Documentation:

APA requires in-text citation of sources. These citations allow readers to locate the source information on the References page.

In-text citations require three types of information: the **author's last name** and the **year of publication** must always appear with borrowed information. The third type of information, **the page number**(s), is required only for direct quotations.

Examples:

For borrowed information (not a quotation)

(Brown, 2006)
(Dailey, 2005)

It is very difficult to be objective when editing your own writing (Williams, 2007).

OR for direct quotations

(Brown, 2006, p. 159)
(Dailey, 2005, pp. 176-179)

In order to edit your own work, you must learn "to diagnose your prose in ways that sidestep your intractable subjectivity" (Williams, 2007, p. 133).

Note: Use "p." before single page numbers and "pp." before multiple pages.

In-Text Documentation - General Rules

If you are paraphrasing from a source, you are encouraged but not required to include the page number in your documentation.

Placement of In-Text Documentation:

Several options exist for integrating in-text citations. Below are some common ways that you can include this information in the body of your paper.

1. The most common way to introduce a citation is with a "signal phrase" that includes the author's name.

Examples:

According to Honan (1987), Jane Austen had a romantic interest in Tom Lefroy.

In Foer's latest novel (2005), young Oskar finds a key belonging to his deceased father.

2. If you have used a signal phrase for a quote, give the page number at the end of the quotation.

Examples:

According to Honan (1987), Austen's "flirting had been guided by her squeezing of a situation for possibilities never in it" (p. 110).

Foer (2005) paints Oskar as a creative, yet troubled child, with ideas for new inventions including "mencils" and "birdseed shirts" (p. 71).

In-Text Documentation - General Rules

3. If the author's name is not in the signal phrase, enclose it in parentheses at the end of the information.

Example:

Jane Austen had a romantic interest in Tom Lefroy (Honan, 1987).

If you have used a direct quote, give the page number as well.

Example:

Austin's "flirting had been guided by her squeezing of a situation for possibilities never in it" (Honan, 1987, p. 110).

Documenting Paragraphs:

1. Documentation does not need to be repeated for every idea within a single paragraph. For example, if you retrieved information for three consecutive sentences from the same source, you can put the information after the third sentence.

Example:

Jane Austen may have met Tom Lefroy at Ashe or at the Harwood's ball. She was twenty at the time. Austen admired Lefroy's conservative nature and decided to fall in love with him (Honan, 1987).

In-Text Documentation - General Rules

2. If you mention an author's name more than once in a paragraph, give the year after the first mention, but not after subsequent references within the paragraph.

Example:

According to Honan (1987), Tom Lefroy went to live with his aunt for a much needed rest. At this time, he was nearly 20, well-dressed and quiet. Honan suggests that Lefroy came off as dim-witted.

---

3. If you mention a source, and later in the paragraph use information from the same source, you can add just the page number, and that indicates to the reader that you are referencing the preceding source.

Example:

According to Honan (1987), Austen's "pride had kept her from seeing him as a baffling person with plans uninvolved with her imaginings" (p. 111). Two years later, when Lefroy's aunt spoke about him, Austen was obstinate and proud. She did not ask about him at all. She was "perplexed by her own obstinacy" (p. 111).

Finally, when you move from one paragraph to the next, you must repeat source information, even if you are using the same source.

In-Text Documentation - General Rules

Long Quotations (40+ Words):

If a quotation is longer than 40 words, start the quote on a new line, indenting the entire quote five spaces on the left margin. Do not justify the right margin. **Do not use quotation marks**. Double space all. Close the quote with a period and then the documentation in parenthesis.

Example:

Jonathan Safran Foer (2005) conveys Oskar's "ah-ha"

moment in the following passage:

> Why hadn't Mom said anything?
>
> Or done anything?
>
> Or cared at all?
>
> And then, all of a sudden, it made perfect sense.
>
> All of a sudden I understood why, when Mom asked where I was going, and I said "Out," she didn't ask any more questions. She didn't have to because she knew. (291)

Note: If the quote is more than one paragraph, indent the beginning of additional paragraphs five spaces. The above example shows five paragraphs.

In-Text Documentation - Common Problems

1. The source does not have an author. Use the title of the article or book in place of the author. Use quotes around the title of an article and italicize the title of a book. Use regular title capitalization (note: this is different from the References page). You can also give the title in the body of your paper and the page number in parentheses.

Examples:

The theory of Multiple Intelligences, proposed by Howard Gardner, has been utilized by a variety of educators ("Multiple Intelligences," 2002).

Educators around the world are using Multiple Intelligences Theory to help students "discover new, more effective ways of learning" ("Multiple Intelligences," 2005, para. 2).

2. The work has two authors. Give both authors in the body of the paper or in the parenthetical (in parentheses) documentation. Use "&" between the names in the parenthetical documentation. Give the date (and page number for a quotation).

Examples:

We can identify students with high linguistic intelligence as those who learn best by speaking, hearing or seeing words (Beachner & Picket, 2001).

In-Text Documentation - Common Problems

> According to Beachner and Pickett (2001), students with high linguistic intelligence tend to "think in words rather than pictures" (p. 17).

3. The work has three to five authors. The first time you mention the source, give all authors in the body of the paper or in the parenthetical documentation. Use "&" between the last two names, and follow with the date.

Example of 1st mention:

> It is better to print a copy of your paper than to attempt to edit on screen (Ruszkiewicz, Friend, & Hairston, 2007).

In subsequent references, give only the first author's name and date (and page number if quoting) followed by the phrase "et al." (meaning "and others").

Example of subsequent use:

> One effective way to edit your own work is to read it out loud (Ruskiewicz et al., 2007).

OR

> Ruszkiewicz et al. (2007) offer several helpful suggestions on editing your own work.

In-Text Documentation - Common Problems

4. The work has six or more authors. Give the first author's name followed by "et al." either in the body of the paper or in the parenthetical documentation.

Examples:

The ethical issues of stem cell use are addressed in the essay entitled "The Ethical Validity of Using Nuclear Transfer in Human Transplantation" (Lanza et al., 2000).

Or:

Lanza et al. (2000) discuss the ethical issues of stem cell use in their essay, "The Ethical Validity of Using Nuclear Transfer in Human Transplantation."

5. A group or organization is the author. Use the name of the organization in place of the author. Each time your reference the source, give the date, then the page number if required.

Examples:

Gardening can help kids develop social skills, develop bonds in families, understand nature and more (American Horticultural Society, 2007).

According to American Council on Exercise (2007), strength training is a vital part of maintaining bone density.

6. Two or more works have the same author and the same publication year. Label the works a, b, etc. after the year and include those letters in the in-text documentation. Be sure the same labels are applied on the References page.

Examples:

Schachner (2007a) **or** (Schachner, 2007a)

Schachner (2007b) **or** (Schachner, 2007b)

---

7. Your author is anonymous. Use the word "Anonymous" in place of the author's name, both in-text and on the References page. Note that this is for a source designated as anonymous, **not** for a work without an author (see #1, above).

Example:

(Anonymous, 2006)

---

8. Your source doesn't have page numbers. Often information retrieved from the Internet will not have page numbers. Do not include the page numbers that appear on your printout. Instead, give your reader information that will help him or her locate the passage. If the paragraphs are numbered, use the abbreviation para. followed by the number. If there are no page numbers and no paragraph numbers, include a heading and the number of the paragraph after that heading to help the reader find the material.

For example, if one of the headings in your source is "Developing Lines of Communication," use this parenthetical citation:

("Developing Lines of Communication," para. 3)

If a heading is very long, you may shorten it for the parenthetical reference. For example, if the heading is "Teaching Methods of Whole Language and Phonics Combine for the Most Effective Results," you could use this parenthetical citation:

("Teaching Methods of Whole Language," para. 2).

9. You are documenting an interview or other personal communication. Interviews, e-mails and other personal communications are not retrievable by your reader. Therefore, these works are not included on the References page. Instead, these sources are documented in-text. Include the person's name, the words "personal communication," and the full date of the communication. The name can be included in the body of the text, or in the parenthetical reference.

Examples:

(S. Mitchell, personal communication, March 14, 2009)

Or

According to Steven Mitchell (personal communication, March 14, 2009), a variety of methods for treating the disease are available.

If you use the source again in your paper, you do not need to repeat the words "personal communication." Give only last name and year in subsequent documentation.

10. You use two different sources for the same information or in the same part of the paper. Put both sources in the same parenthetical documentation. To do this, include the author's last name and date in parenthesis in alphabetical order by the first author's last name. The sources should be listed in the same order that they are found on the References page. Separate the citations with semi-colons.

Examples:

Several essays (Campbell, 1989; Checkley, 1997; Holmes, 2002) examine the use of "Multiple Intelligences" in the classroom.

The connection between bone mass and strength training has been proven repeatedly (Andreoli, et al., 2001;Picard, Imback, Coutuier, Lepage, & Ste-Marie, 2004; Proctor, et al., 2000; Rutherford, 1999).

Style

Common Style Issues:

1. What if my quote quotes someone else?

This is called a quote within a quote. Use double quotation marks to start your quote then single quotation marks around the part quoted by your source.

> **Example:**
> "Jim Jones sees many problems with the regulators. 'They will do massive damage,' he asserts."

2. Should I use 1 space after a period or 2?

Use one space after a period in References and one space after periods in names (J. C. Brown, for example). Use two spaces after punctuation marks that end a sentence.

3. Should I use italics or quotation marks around titles?

APA specifies italics for titles of books, movies, television broadcasts, television series, music albums and journals. Use quotation marks around titles of journal articles, television series episodes, and short stories.

> **Example:**
> *The Grapes of Wrath* is a novel that many students read in high school.

Style

4. Does the period go inside or outside the quotation marks?

If you are not providing documentation information, the period goes inside the quotes.

> **Example:**
>
> Bob said, "Several people have attempted this climb."

However, if you are providing documentation in parentheses, the period comes after the parentheses.

> **Example:**
>
> Jane Austen was "left with her reflections in 1796" (Honan, 1987, p. 110).

5. When and how do I use ellipses (...)?

Ellipses are used to indicate that information has been omitted. Do not use ellipses at the beginning or end of a quotation. Use 3 periods for ellipses, or 4 if you need to include a period.

6. When should I use brackets ([ ])?

Use brackets within a quote when you need to add information for clarification or explanation, or to indicate a mistake is not your own [sic].

7. How do I handle headings?

Headings are optional. For undergraduate papers, use only one level of headings. Center the headings, and capitalize all major words. Many papers written in behavioral and social sciences utilize headings.

Style

8. What should I do with figures, tables, graphs and charts?

The APA Manual contains an entire chapter (Chapter 5 "Displaying Results," 42 pages) explaining how to use graphs and charts. If you are presenting your own research in this manner, we recommend that you consult the APA Manual. All figures, tables, graphs and charts should have a function in your paper. Do not include them if they are not necessary.

9. Should I write out numbers?

Use figures to express numbers 10 and above. Use words for numbers below 10.

Examples:				
one	two	nine percent	10%	27 years old

10. Should I use footnotes?

You may use footnotes to supplement the information in the text. In most cases, it is best to try to integrate the information into the body of the paper instead. Do not use footnotes for documentation. Here are some general rules about footnotes:

* Include footnotes only if they help your discussion.

* Keep footnotes brief.

* Each footnote should contain only one idea.

* Number all footnotes in the order in which they appear in your paper.

General Guidelines for References

The References page provides the information your readers need to access the sources used in your paper (see model, p. 17). Follow these general guidelines:

1. The References list must include all sources cited directly in the paper. Do not include sources not cited.

2. List your sources alphabetically by the author's last name.

3. Double space all entries and indent all entry lines, excluding the first line (called hanging indent).

4. If you have more than one work by exactly the same author(s), list the one with the earliest publication date first. If both have the same date, list the works alphabetically by title, and add "a" and "b" after the year: (2002a) and (2002b), for example.

Note: You must use these same alphabetized dates in the in-text documentation.

5. Never put quotation marks around titles on the References page.

6. Do not split entries from one page to the next. If you do not have enough room on the page to complete the entry, move the entire entry to the next page.

References Page - Digital Object Identifiers

7. Personal communications, including interviews, e-mail, telephone interviews, etc. are not considered retrievable information and, therefore, are not listed on the References page. See p. 27 on how to document these sources in-text.

Digital Object Identifiers (DOI):

One of the main problems with Internet sources has been their lack of consistency. A link that works today may not work tomorrow, and in such cases, readers of your paper cannot access your sources.

In an effort to combat this problem, the APA manual suggests that writers use the Digital Object Identifier (DOI) when documenting Internet sources. The DOI is a unique string of letters and numbers that identifies the source and provides a link to that source that will not change over time. If you identify the DOI in your References, you can be sure that the number will provide a link to your source now and in the future.

Finding the DOI:

The DOI is usually on the first page of the document near the copyright information. The DOI may be hidden; look for a link labeled Article, PubMed, CrossRef or other vendor name.

For help with DOI, visit http://doi.org/ To look up a DOI number, visit http://www.crossref.org/and use the Guest Query form.

References Page - DOI

The DOI in References:

When available, the DOI takes the place of the Internet or database address. The DOI is always documented in the same manner: replace "Retrieved from" and the Internet or database address at the end of the reference with: "doi:" and the DOI number. See the sample formats shown below.

Format (books with Internet address):
Last Name, Initial(s). (year). *Title of book.* [Information about digital version.] Retrieved from address.

Format (books using DOI number):
Last Name, Initial(s). (year). *Title of book.* [Information about digital version.] doi: number.

Common Problems with the DOI:

1. If you find a DOI and it is not a live link, it is a good idea to go to crossref.org and type in the DOI. If the DOI is valid, your article will appear on the page. You should always try to find a DOI for a Internet source and always give the DOI if you find one.

2. If the document does not have a DOI, you should give the URL (the address for the page). In many cases (particularly for databases and magazines), it is recommended that you give the address for the entry page with the understanding that a search tool on the site will enable your reader to access the article.

References Page - Books

Books:

Instructions:

1. Begin with the author's **last name**, a comma, then his or her **initials** (first and middle if available, each followed by a period).

2. List the **year** of publication in parenthesis followed by a period.

3. Give the **title of the book** in italics. Capitalize only the first word of the title, proper nouns, and the first word after a colon or dash (if any). End the title with a period.

4. Identify the **city and state** (two letter state abbreviation: for example, FL) or **city and country** of publication, followed by a colon. American cities commonly known for publishing do not require a state abbreviation (Baltimore, Boston, Chicago, Los Angeles, New York, Philadelphia, and San Francisco). Likewise, the following international cities do not require a country name: Amsterdam, Jerusalem, London, Milan, Moscow, Paris, Rome, Stockholm, Tokyo, and Vienna.

5. Finally, give the name of the publisher, followed by a period.

Format:
Last Name, Initial(s). (year). *Title of book.* City:
　　Publisher.

References Page - Electronic Version of a Book

Examples:

Brown, J. C. (1999). *Sleep deprivation: Problems and
solutions.* Los Angeles: Harper Collins.

Davis, C. (2005). *Season of the snake.* New York: St.
Martin's Press.

Electronic Version of a Book:

Use this model for both the electronic version of
a print book OR an electronic-only book.

Instructions:

1. Give the author, date and title as for a print
version of a book.

2. If you have information about the digital version,
include it in brackets (for example, Adobe
Digital Editions version).

3. Follow with the words "Retrieved from" and the
Internet address OR follow with "doi:" and the
number for the book (see information on DOI on
page 33).

4. If the book is an electronic version republished
from a print version, include that information in
parentheses).

Format (using the Internet address):

Last Name, Initial(s). (year). *Title of book.* [Information
about digital version.] Retrieved from address.

References Page - Common Problems

Examples:

Austen, J. (1905). *Persuasion.* [Winchester edition]. Retrieved
from http://www.archive.org/details/persuasion00austuoft

Sewell, A. (2006). *Black beauty.* [eBook #271, transcribed from
1811 edition]. Retrieved from http://www.gutenberg.org

OR

Format (using DOI number):

Last Name, Initial(s). (year). *Title of book.* [Information
about digital version.] doi: number.

Examples:

Tang, L. C., Goh, T. N., Yam, H. S., & Yoap, T. (Eds.). (2006).
Six Sigma. New York: Wiley & Sons. doi: 10.1002/
0470062002

El-Haik, B., & Roy, D. M. (2005). *Service design for Six Sigma.*
New York: Wiley & Sons. doi:10.1002/0471744719

Common Problems:

1. Missing initials. You may not always be able to
give the first and middle initial. In this case, give the
information you have (see following example).

2. Multiple authors. For up to seven authors, list the
authors, last name first, with initials, in the same
order they appear on your original source. Separate
the names with commas and an ampersand (&)
before the last name. For more than seven
authors, see page 47 in journal section.

For more than seven authors, see page 47 in journal section.

37

References Page - Common Problems

Example:

Patterson, K., Grenny, J., McMillan, R., & Switzler, A. (2005).
   Crucial confrontations: Tools for resolving broken
   promises, violated expectations, and bad behavior. New
   York: McGraw-Hill.

3. More than one date on the copyright page of the text. If several dates are listed, cite the original publication date. If the book is a revised edition, use the date of revision.

4. An editor instead of an author. Give name of the editor(s), then Ed. or Eds. in parentheses, followed by a period.

Example:

Rosen, M. (Ed.). (1985). *The Kingfisher book of children's*
   poetry. Boston: Kingfisher Publications.

5. A group, committee, or corporation as author. Use the name of the group or organization in place of the author. Alphabetize accordingly.

Example:

Academy of American Poets. (1984). *Fifty years of American*
   poetry: Over 200 important works by America's modern
   masters. New York: Dell Publishing.

References Page - Common Problems

6. Edition other than the first. Add the number of the edition with letters "ed." in parentheses after the title.

> **Example:**
>
> Bertoline, G. R., Wiebe, E. N., & Wiebe, E. (2002). *Technical graphics communication.* (3rd ed.). New York: McGraw-Hill.
>
> Williams, J. M. (2007). *Style: Lessons in clarity and grace.* (9th ed.). New York: Pearson Education.

7. A chapter or selection from a book or anthology. List the author of the section or part, then the date of publication of the book, followed by the section or chapter title. Next, give the word "In" followed by the title of the book (in italics) and the page numbers for the chapter or section in parentheses (use pp. before the page numbers). Finally, give the city and publisher as with a standard book entry.

> **Example:**
>
> Gavell, M.L. (2001). The swing. In *I cannot tell a lie, exactly* (pp. 3-16). New York: Random House.

Journals: Paper Copy

Instructions:

1. Begin with the author's last name, a comma, then his or her initials (first and middle if available, each followed by a period).

2. List the year of publication in parenthesis, followed by a period. DO NOT give the month or day if the journal has a volume number.

3. Give the title of the article. Capitalize only the first word of the title, proper nouns, and the first word after a colon (if any). End the title with a period. Do not use quotation marks; do not italicize or underline the title of the article.

4. Give the title of the journal. Follow normal title capitalization rules. Italicize and follow with a comma.

5. Give the volume number; follow with a comma, all italicized. Give issue number if the journal is paginated by issue (each issue begins with page 1) in parenthesis after the volume (not italicized).

6. Cite the page numbers (not italicized).

Format:

Last Name, Initial(s). (year). Title of article. *Title of Periodical, volume number*(issue number), page numbers.

Examples:

Smith, J. T. (2004). Overcoming sleep disorders. *Journal of the American Medical Association, 82,* 293-298.

Chin, L., Garraway, L. A., & Fisher, D. E. (2006). Malignant Melanoma: Genetics and therapeutic in the genomic era. *Genes & Development, 20,* 2149-2182.

Journal Article (online)

With DOI---

If you retrieved your article online and have the DOI, follow the above instructions for the paper journal. After the page number, type the letters "doi" (all lower case), followed by a colon and the number. Do NOT use a final period at the end of the entry.

Format:

Last Name, Initial(s). (year). Title of article. *Title of Periodical, volume number*(issue number), page numbers. doi: number

Examples:

Chin, L., Garraway, L. A., & Fisher, D. E. (2006). Malignant melanoma: Genetics and therapeutic in the genomic era. *Genes & Development, 20,* 2149-2182. doi: 10.1101/gad.1437206

References Page - Journals, Magazines, Newspapers

Baum, M.A., & Groeling, T. (2008). New media and the
polarization of American political discourse. *Political
Communication, 25*(4), 345. doi: 10.1080/
10584600802426965

Without DOI--

If you retrieved your article online and the DOI is
not available, follow the instructions for the paper
journal. After the page numbers, give the words
"Retrieved from" (capital R, no punctuation) followed
by the URL of the journal's home page. Do not give
the retrieval date.

Format:

Last Name, Initial(s). (year). Title of article. *Title of
Periodical, volume number*(issue number), page
numbers. Retrieved from address.

Examples:

Barolsky, P. (2006). Ovid's Protean epic of art. *Arion: A
Journal of Humanities and the Classics, 14*(1), 111-123.
Retrieved from http://www.bu.edu/arion/

Shen, J. & Eder, L.B. (2009). Intentions to use virtual worlds
for education. *Journal of Information Systems Education,
20*(2), 225-234. Retrieved from
http://www.jise.appstate.edu/

References Page - Journals, Magazines, Newspapers

Journal article from a database—

If you retrieved your article from a database and the article has a DOI, follow the instructions for DOI on page 43. If the article does not have a DOI and is not easily located through its primary publication, give the URL for the entry page of the online database.

Format:

Last Name, Initial(s). (year). Title of article. *Title of Periodical, volume number*(issue number), page numbers. doi: number

Example:

Falcomata, T., Northup, J., Dutt, A., Stricker, J., Vinquist, K., & Engebretson, B. (2008). A preliminary analysis of instructional control in the maintenance of appropriate behavior. *Journal of Applied Behavior Analysis, 41*(3), 429-34. doi:10.1901/jaba.2008.41-429

OR

Format:

Last Name, Initial(s). (year). Title of article. *Title of Periodical, volume number*(issue number), page numbers. Retrieved from address

Example:

Lane, H., Pullen, P., Hudson, R., & Konold, T. (2009). Identifying essential instructional components of literacy tutoring for struggling beginning readers. *Literacy Research and Instruction, 48*(4), 277-297. Retrieved from http://www.proquest.com/en-US/

Magazine article (paper)

Follow the same format as for paper journal; however, give the full date of the article (year, then month). Give the volume number and issue number if available.

> **Format:**
> Last Name, Initial(s). (year, month). Title of article. *Title of Magazine*, page numbers.

> **Examples:**
> Layton, R. (2007, July/August). Missteps beget mishaps: Improper procedures compromise safety. *Alert Diver*, 41-43.
> Caillot, A. (2008/2009, Winter). The way we work. *Creative Kids, 27*, 12.

Magazine article (online)

Follow the same format as for the magazine article. After citation information, add the words "Retrieved from" (capital R, no punctuation) and the address of the home page of the magazine. Do not put a period after the address.

> **Format:**
> Last Name, Initial(s). (year, month). Title of article. *Title of Magazine*. Retrieved from Internet address

References Page

Examples:

Dunn, R. (2009, August). The culture of being rude. *Smithsonian.com*. Retrieved from http://www.smithsonianmag.com/

Mayer, C. (2009, November 19). British support for Afghan war fades. *Time.com*. Retrieved from http://www.time.com/time/

Newspaper article (paper)

Follow the same format as for a magazine with these changes: 1) include the full date in parentheses, and 2) list the page number preceded by a p. (pp. for multiple pages). Give numbers of all pages on which the article appears.

Note: Newspapers often have a section number (or letter) and a page number (for example, A12 or 16.5).

Format:

Last Name, Initial(s). (year, month day). Title of article. *Title of Newspaper*, p. (or pp.) page numbers.

Examples:

King, C. (1996, October 26). Corrupt at corrections. *The Washington Post*, p. A23.

Stefanakis, E. H. (2006, January 8). Failing our students. *New York Times*, p. 14.13.

Newspaper article (online)

Follow the rules for a newspaper. After the name of the newspaper, add the address for the home page of the paper.

Format:

Last Name, Initial(s). (year, month day). Title of article.
Title of Newspaper. Retrieved from Internet address
of home page

Examples:

Hernandez, J.C. (2009, September 15). A new meaning for
cutting classes. *The New York Times*. Retrieved from
http://www.nytimes.com

Vergano, D. (2009, November 19). Ancient crocodiles diverse:
Some ate dinosaurs. *USAToday.com*. Retrieved from
http://www.usatoday.com/

(**Common Problems:**)

1. Missing initials. If you don't have first and/or middle initials, give the information you have.

2. Editorial without an author. Use the word Editorial in place of the author's name, followed by a colon. Next, give the title of the editorial followed by the word Editorial in brackets. Give the date and the rest of the publication information.

Example:

Editorial: Seven years after the sniper. [Editorial]. (2009, September 30). *New York Times*. Retrieved from http://www.nytimes.com

3. Multiple authors (2-7 authors). For two to seven authors, list the authors, last name first, with initials, in the same order they appear on your original source. Separate the names by commas, with an ampersand (&) before the last name.

Example:

Visser, B. A., Ashton, M. C., & Vernon, P. A. (2006). Beyond G: Putting Multiple Intelligences Theory to the test. *Intelligence, 34,* 487 (16).

4. For more than seven authors, list the first six authors as explained above, followed by a comma, three ellipses, and the last author (last name first, then initials) followed by a period.

Examples:

Jabbour, E., Hosing, C., Ayers, G., Nunez, R., Anderlini, P., Pro, B., . . . Fayad, L. (2007). Pretransplant positive positron emission tomography/gallium scans predict poor outcome in patients with recurrent/refractory Hodgkin lymphoma. *Cancer, 109,* 2481-2490.

Denis, L., Namey, M., Costello, K., Frenette, J., Gagnon, N.,
Harris, C., . . . Poirier, J. (2004). Long-term treatment
optimization in individuals with Multiple Sclerosis using
disease-modifying therapies: A nursing approach. *Journal
of Neuroscience Nursing, 36,* 10-22. doi:10.1097/
01376517-200402000- 000033.

5. Journals paginated issue by issue vs. continuous pagination. Some journals begin with page one in issue one, and continue the second issue where the first ended (referred to as continuous pagination). Others are paginated issue by issue (that is, they begin with page one on each issue). For journal articles paginated issue by issue, include the issue number.

Example:

Evans, C. (1995). Access, equity and intelligence: Another look at tracking. *English Journal, 84*(8), 63-66.

For journals with continuous pagination, you only need the volume number.

Example:

Levin, H. M. (1994). Commentary: Multiple Intelligence Theory and everyday practices. *Teachers College Record, 95,* 570-576.

Online and Electronic Resources

The APA manual has a very small section on electronic resources. Most electronic resources are included in other sections of the book. For example, the format for documenting an online journal article is included in the journals section. We have followed the same format in this guide but included charts for cross reference.

Below are examples of resources commonly accessed online.

Internet Message Boards and Online Forums, Blogs, and Electronic Mailing Lists:

1. Begin with the author's last name, a comma, then his or her initials (first and middle if available, each followed by a period).

2. List the date (year, month day) of posting in parentheses.

3. Give the message subject line. Capitalize only the first word, proper nouns, and the first word after a colon, if any. End with a period. Do not use italics.

4. Give a description of the message in brackets.

5. Give the words "Retrieved from" followed by the full address for the archived message.

Format:
Last, Initial(s). (date). Title of post [Description of the format]. Retrieved from address

References Page - Online and Electronic Resources

Forum/Discussion Group Examples:

Tippytoes. (2009, October 29). Re: More pins and needles
    [Online forum comment]. Retrieved from
    http://tabletalk.salon.com/webx/.773b559b

QTE (U14012755). (2009, October 16). Perversion of belief?
    [Online forum comment]. Retrieved from
    http://www.bbc.co.uk/dna/mbreligion/
    F2213233?thread=700156

Blog Examples:

Lunt, S. (2007, July 14). Wrangellers [Web log post]. Retrieved
    from http://shaunlunt.typepad.com/

Bearnson, L. (2009, November 19). Hold on, the light will come!
    [Web log post]. Retrieved from
    http://www.lisabearnson.com/blog/

Other Internet documents:

Try to find a category for your online documents. For example, if your online document is an article from a journal, use the model for online journals. However, if your online document does not fit into any of the categories listed, use the following general rules, models and examples.

Instructions:

1. If the document or page has an author, list that name first. If the document was written by a group or organization, list that as the author.

2. Scan the site for a date of publication or last update. Include that date. If no date is available, use n.d. in parentheses in place of the date.

3. If the document is part of a larger work, give the title of the document first, without italics or quotation marks. Then give the word "In" followed by the title of the whole work in italics.

4. If the document stands alone, give the title in italics.

5. Give the words "Retrieved from" followed by the address for the document.

Format:

Last name, Initial(s). (date). Title of document. In *Title of complete work*. Retrieved from address.

Or

Last name, Initial(s). (date). *Title of document.* Retrieved from address.

Examples:

The National Institutes of Health. (2009). *Stem cell basics.* Retrieved from http://stemcells.nih.gov/info/basics/

Becoming a green business. (2009). Retrieved from http://www.go-green.com/node/144

Other Resources --

Technical and Government Reports

Technical and government reports are most commonly accessed online. When documenting such reports from a paper source, simply omit the address.

Instructions:

1. The organization issuing the report is the author unless an individual author is listed.

2. If the organization labels the report with a number, give that number in parentheses after the title.

3. Documents from the U.S. Government Printing Office should be identified clearly. List the location as Washington, D.C., and the publisher as Government Printing Office.

4. If the publisher is not the author, give publisher information just before the address:
Retrieved from Name of Agency Internet site: address.

Format:

Organization or author. (date). *Title of work* (number assigned by organization). Location: Publisher. Retrieved from address

---

References Page

Example:

U.S. Environmental Protection Agency. (2004). *Guide to purchasing green power* (EPA430-K-04-015). Washington, D.C.: U.S. Environmental Protection Agency. Retrieved from http://www.epa.gov/grnpower/documents/ purchasing_guide_for_web.pdf

Audiovisual Materials:

This category includes podcasts and other online videos, as well as maps, movies, music and art. Give the main contributor as the author and identify that person's role in parentheses. After the title, indicate the type of media in brackets.

Online Sources:

Format:

Last name, Initial(s) (Job Title). (year, month day). Title of work [type of media]. Retrieved from address.

Podcast Examples:

Sloan, R. (Producer). (2009, December 10). *Moving voices 2009 special edition* [audio podcast]. Retrieved from http://www.podcastdirectory.com/podshows/6268675

Treisman, D. (Fiction Editor). (2009, December 15). *Junot Diaz reads Edwidge Danticat* [audio podcast]. Retrieved from http://www.learnoutloud.com/Podcast-Directory/Literature/ Contemporary-Literature/The-New-Yorker-Fiction- Podcast/28347#plink

Map Example:

Good, J. (Cartographer). (1793). Plan of the city of
Washington [Road map]. Retrieved from
http://www.dcvote.org/trellis/character/maps/35.jpg

Movies:

List the major contributors such producers and
directors.

Format:

Last name, Initial(s) (Producer), & Last name, Initial(s)
(Director). (year). *Title of movie* [Motion picture].
Country of Origin: Studio.

Examples:

Landau, J. (Producer), & Cameron, J. (Director). (2009).
Avatar [Motion picture]. United States: 20th Century
Fox.

Selznick, D.O. (Producer) & Fleming, V. (Director). (1939).
Gone with the wind [Motion picture]. United States:
Warner Brothers Entertainment.

Music:

Begin the entry with the name of the song writer. If the writer and the performer of the song are not the same, include "Recorded by" and the performer's initials and last name in brackets after the title of the song.

Format:

Last name, Initial(s). (Year of copyright). Title of song [Recorded by Initials Last Name]. On *Title of Album* [Type of recording]. Location: Label. (Date of recording if different from copyright date).

Note: If writer and performer are the same, omit [Recorded by Initials Last Name].

Example:

Crow, C. (2005). Always on your side. On *Wildflower* [CD]. New York: A&M Records.

Mayer, J. & LaBruyere, D. (2003). Home life [Recorded by J. Mayer]. On *Heavier things* [CD]. New York: Columbia Records.

Reviews (of books, films, etc.)

Begin with the name of the reviewer. In brackets, give information about the reviewed item: "Review of" followed by the genre (book, film, video game), the word "by," and the author of the reviewed item.

Format:

Last, Initial(s). (date). Title of review [Review of the book/film/video/video game *Title of book/film/video/video game,* by author of book/film/video/video game]. *Title of work containing review, volume,* page numbers. AND/OR Retrieved from Internet address

Book Review Example:

Updike, J. (2005, March 14). Mixed messages [Review of the book *Extremely Loud and Incredibly Close,* by J.S. Foer]. *The New Yorker.* Retrieved from http://www.newyorker.com/archive/2005/03/14/050314crbo_books1

Film Review Example:

Alter, E. (2009, December 15). Film review: *Avatar* [Review of the film *Avatar,* produced by Jon Landau, 2009]. Retrieved from http://www.filmjournal.com/filmjournal/content_display/reviews/ major-releases/e3if667a78777fe70e11f6c65ca8ba655c9

Additional Resources

Additional Resources:

The following Internet sites may be helpful as you work on APA documentation:

http://apastyle.apa.org

http://uca.edu/writingcenter/documents/
   APA.style.pdf

http://owl.english.purdue.edu/owl/

For complete and specific rules on APA documentation, consult *The Publication Manual of the American Psychological Association* (6th ed., 2nd printing), ISBN 1-4338-0561-8

Index

Format:
Abstract page 12-13
General 8-9
References page 16-17
Text page 14-15
Title page 10-11

In-Text Documentation:
Anonymous author 26
Basic models 18
Group as author 25
Interviews 27-28
Long quotes 22
Missing page numbers 26-27
Multiple sources in
  a single documentation 28
No author 23
Paragraphs 20-21
Six or more authors 25
Three to five authors 24
Two authors 23-24
Two or more works by
  the same author 26

Style:
Charts, tables, graphs 31
Brackets 30
Ellipses 30
Footnotes 31
Headings 30
Italics 29
Numbers 31
Period placement 30
Quote within a quote 29
Spacing 29

Index

References:
  General Guidelines 32

Books:
  Basic book entry 35-36
  Chapter 39
  Edited 38
  Edition 39
  Electronic 36-37
  Group as author 38
  Missing initials 37
  Multiple authors 37
  Multiple dates 38

Journals:
  Basic journal 40
  Electronic journal 41-42
    Database 43
    Online 41
  Missing initials 46
  More than 7 authors 47
  Multiple authors 47
  Paginated by issue 48
  Paginated continuously 48

Internet sites:
  Audiovisual material 53-55
  Electronic mailing list 49
  Map 54
  Message board 49
  Other Internet documents 50-51
  Podcast 53
  Web Log (blog) 49-50

Miscellaneous sources:
  Government report 52
  Magazine article 44-45
  Movie 54
  Music 55
  Newspaper article 45-46
  Review 56